HELPING EMPLOYEES EMBRACE CHANGE

Change Management Tips for Managers

Ifra Publication

The characters and events portrayed in this book are fictitious. Any similarity to real persons, living or dead, is coincidental and not intended by the author.

CONTENTS

WHAT YOU'LL LEARN

1. How to own your role in change situations
2. How to effectively listen to your team
3. How to collaborate to win
4. How to help build productive perspective
5. How to manage reactions to change
6. How to support positivity and wellness

ABOUT

There is constant change, and it appears to attack us from all sides. You will study techniques to help you become more adaptable, agile, and open to change in this Book, Helping Employees Embrace Change. This capacity is crucial to help you stay relevant in your line of work and in your professional environment.

When you grasp the "why" underlying your resistance to change, you will be better able to adapt to and grow through the change you encounter. First, you will learn to appreciate the benefit of change.

You will next learn the benefits of having a growth mindset and how it can keep you curious and receptive to unexpected change. Finally, you will examine the most typical changes to your workplace and the abilities that will best enable you to adapt to them.

You will have gained new knowledge by the end of this Book that, if put to use, will help you stay adaptable, nimble, and better equipped to handle and grow from change in both your professional and personal lives.

WHO THIS BOOK IS FOR

1. Professionals of all varieties who wish to become leaders.
2. Established leaders who want to improve their effectiveness at work.
3. Executives and senior leaders who need a refresher about helping employees deal with change.

INTRODUCTION

Hello. My name is Ifra. I am a business leader. I have over 22 years of leadership experience. Welcome to my Book, Helping Employees Embrace Change. Change is everywhere, companies, organisations, and industries where we work are feeling increased pressures with new regulations, developments, and technology, automation, machine learning, globalisation, and changing demographics.

Now this Book is not designed as a change management Book. There are thousands of courses and articles already available to help guide you through leading change. This Book is designed for you, the individual adult learner. Learnings will be shared to help you become more agile and flexible and open to change as this helps you stay relevant in your profession and your business environments. Some of the major skill sets we will cover in this Book are recognizing the value of change.

We'll review why as humans we tend to fear or avoid change. Once we realise why we shy away from change, we become more adept at adapting and growing with the change we face. I'll be teaching the value of having a growth mindset and how this helps us stay curious and open-minded to unexpected change. I'll share with you the most common changes to expect in your work environment and teach you skills that will best help you navigate through these changes.

By the end of this Book, you will have learned new skills that, if implemented, will help keep you agile and flexible and better able to handle the changes that each of us constantly face. Learnings in this Book will not only help us show up more positively and impactful in our work environments, but if used, they will also help us adapt and become more agile with the change we face in our personal lives as well.

I hope you'll join me on this journey of learning, embracing change, staying agile in the midst of change here at Amazon.

THE VALUE OF EMBRACING CHANGE

Change is everywhere. Companies, organisations, and industries where we work are feeling increased pressures with new regulations, developments in technology, automation, machine learning, globalisation, and along with this the ever-changing demographics. Hello, my name is Ifra. Thank you for reading this Book, Helping Employees Embrace Change.

I have over 22 years of senior-level leadership experience in both business management and human resources, supporting multiple technology companies. One of my many leadership passions is helping individuals stay fluid and relevant in the midst of the constant change that takes place all around us. In this Book, we will be learning about coping with change. As humans, we are predictably resistant to change and we are biologically hardwired to our habits, and these two innate human responses often show detrimental to our careers and our professional growth due to the ever-changing world around us.

Change is everywhere. Resistance is futile. Eventually we will all be assimilated, right? In my professional career, I remember the Tuesday FedEx package that came every week from the corporate office crammed with papers, communications, agendas, company directives, newsletters, and oh, so much more. Yes, we killed a lot of trees back in the day, and yep, this was pre-email days. I lived it and I survived it. I also recall when I got my first pager. Nope, not a cell phone, but a pager. Boy was that cool. I walked around with this black box clipped on my belt, anxiously awaiting for the buzz that would let me know I was needed.

I would then quickly exit the freeway, search desperately for the nearest gas station, pre-GPS days as well, and hope I had enough change built up in my car's ashtray to pay for a call. I know it sounds trivial, but wow, these changes really rocked my world. I was a working mom with young kids at home. Knowing that they could page me and I would know to quickly find a payphone to call them back was life changing. Well, for the time. I can go on and on in my self-reflections, remembering my first laptop, receiving email. On dial-up speeds, you only had to wait about 17 minutes to connect and download the emails. Life was exciting.

I know this journey ages me, but it is relevant to our learnings in this Book as it is an example of the journey the human race has been on as we have transitioned into a technology infused world. It's important to note that this Book is not designed as a change management Book. This Book is designed for you, the individual adult learner, to help you become more agile and flexible and open to change. The topics we will be reviewing in this Book are first, the value of embracing change. Next, prepare for unexpected change by living daily with planned change. This learning is essential in helping stabilise ourselves during times of change.

We'll then talk about navigating the challenges of change in your work environments. Here I'll review the most common changes to expect and key skills to help you navigate through those changes. Next, we learned skills to help us become influencers for change. By the end of this Book, you will have learned skill sets that, if implemented, will help keep you agile and flexible to better handle the changes that we consistently face. We all know that there are books and books and books and even more books, and did I say there were books, and articles, blogs, and podcasts that speak to why humans, you and I, resist change.

Most of these books and articles teach that fear is our largest roadblock for all of us to overcome when it comes to handling and dealing with change. In this chapter, we'll learn that it's the fear of change that triggers resistance in humans, stemming mostly from the fear of the unknown. We'll learn the top three reasons why we fear change, as well as three skills to help us face those fears head on. So yes, as humans, we are creatures of habit. We like predictability, and change interferes with our comfort zone.

WHY PEOPLE FEAR CHANGE

Some of the greatest learnings on our fear of change can be found in the studies of neuroleadership. Neuroleadership is best described as an art of synchronising the science of the brain with our behaviours. It is most often used in leadership training as it is said to offer the best hope for affecting real change in people's behaviours. It teaches that uncertainty is what creates a shortage or a gap in our brain functions that registers as tension in the brain. This tension that creates anxiety, worry, and stress is what must be corrected before one can feel comfortable again.

Understanding neuroscience and how it relates to our emotions and behaviours helps us move out of the cerebral intellectual zone and connect logic to our emotions and behaviours. If this concept catches your interest, there are many resources to help you dig a bit deeper into the science of neuroleadership. Back to our teachings around humans' fear of change. I read a statistic once that said over 50% of Americans in their adult lives settle and live within 50 miles of their birthplace. I have a friend who shared with me that in over 50 years of living she had never visited outside the state she was born in.

Crazy sauce when there is such a huge and glorious world to explore and experience. Fear of change not only keeps us from new experiences in our personal lives, but more often than not it is what holds us back in our professional careers. Let's rewind a bit and go back to those most common areas where fear shows up, fear of the unknown, fear of failure, and yes, for some, even that fear of success, fear of rejection, and fear of criticism. Now, tie all of these fears into your professional journey. Have there been promotional opportunities that you've shied away from, maybe volunteer work to lead a project that if you had stepped up it would have improved your own skill set and helped build your personal brand? So many career and advanced learning opportunities are available to us, but most often we will talk ourselves out of reaching for these opportunities due to our fears.

Here are two quick recommendations that help us learn to overcome the fear that keeps us from embracing change. First is to identify the source of the fear for greater understanding. Once we do this, we are more easily equipped to bypass the fear quicker once we recognize the why behind it. Fear can be linked to many causes. For instance, being raised by critical or unsupportive parents is a cause for some people, a past experience with an unsupportive leader or even some previous career failure might be what is triggering the fear. The key is to recognize it and identify the cause. Then once we logically connect why we have these emotions, we are better equipped to change our behaviours to bypass the fear.

My second recommendation is to cryptanalyze, which means to steady it out, break it down to identify as solve. How do you like that word? One of my favourites, I love it. I love crazy awesome words that the word itself just reflects power. Cryptanalyze is a process where you take time to reflect on why you are resisting the change or resisting an opportunity for yourself. Most often it's due to our inner fears. Let's use the example of applying for a new job at work. Reflect on what is causing the fear. Is it fear of taking on additional responsibilities?

Maybe it would put you in a position over peers, peers who have become your friends. It might be if given the job you'd have a new leader you'd report to and that person is unknown to you. This is where you tear it down, dissect the specifics around the fear of the change. Once you've done that, the next step is to visualise solutions for each of these obstacles, identify and dissect the heck out of it, right, get in the nitty gritty as to why you're holding back from embracing the change.

I promise by doing this, it helps work past the fear as your confidence increases now that you've identified solutions to your worries. This tactic has been proven to lessen the worries and anxieties we have regarding change. One of my favourite quotes about fear is feel the fear and do it anyway. Fear can only win and get the best of you if you don't take action and push forward.

OVERCOMING THE FEAR OF CHANGE

Next, we're going to review three reasons why fear is so strongly associated with change. First is fear of the unknown. Humans like predictability. You've heard me say that multiple times already, but let's pause and self-reflect. What are the most common habits that show up day to day for you? Is it that your alarm is set to allow for a 5-minute snooze? Maybe you start each morning at the coffee shop, check email, updates on your phone, maybe a run, a trip to the gym, yoga or a meditation session.

We all have predictable rhythms that show up in our daily routines. We like predictability. Fear of the unknown also shows up in our desire to avoid pain, discomfort, and even effort, a requirement of effort that we wouldn't typically put forth on our own. The second reason why fear shows up so strongly when it comes to change is that often it stems from our low trust or unsurety of the person or situation that is causing the change. This shows up more often in situations where we were not a part of the decision for the change and when the reason for the change is not clearly communicated and explained to gain our buy-in. I know we've all experienced this at some time or another, and some of us are probably experiencing it right now.

I'll spend more time on this issue in chapter four where both leaders and team members can learn to be stronger influencers for change in a more positive way. And the last is one I've already briefly touched on where it shows up in our fear of failure, criticism, and, even for some, fear of success. Now I've already shared two of my personal recommendations to overcome the fear of change, cryptanalyze the situation and identify its origin. I'm now going to quickly share three tips that leadership experts have aligned on as their top three ways to overcome fear that is associated with change.

First, don't accept stability, accept that change is unavoidable. Yes, we know, as humans we are programmed to like predictability, but it's not going to happen, so let's all get our heads around finding the good and joy and power that comes with change. Second is to recognize where that fear comes from. And the third essential step is to live your life as an active adult learner. Our next chapter about living our lives with planned change will dig deeper into this concept. I'm going to take a minute now and lift up that last skill set. Living our lives as active adult learners. This shows up in two different ways.

The first one is to always be learning something new, improving our professional skill set, increasing our knowledge day after day to ensure we stay relevant. The second way this shows up is through living our lives with humility, being open to learn from other people's experiences and to learn from our own experiences as we continue on through life. Do you ever catch yourself doing the same thing over and over and you just want to smack yourself and say really? You know this, why do you keep repeating that behaviour? That's what I mean, learning through our own past experiences. When we see ourselves as a student with life as our teacher, we will be in a constant mode of learning.

Just recently, I came across two situations where I was in the role of coach and tried helping where others were spiralling downward because of their myths of this important concept. I've worked many years in the role of coaching and leading others. In my current leadership role, I spend time with other leaders who are struggling in building a positive culture and environment for their employees. I spend time at their locations. I watch the leader in action. I visit with the leaders' managers and their team members to best help identify why there are culture gaps in their environment. A few months ago I was visiting with one of these struggling leaders.

I was helping to coach him, and as I sat visiting with him with arms folded boldly across his chest, he said to me, I've been doing the same work in the same way for the past 20 years, and that was that. He was clearly stating, I know what I'm doing, I've got this. Who are you to be in here advising me differently? Now in my head I'm thinking dude, you don't have this, you aren't open to the changing landscape around you. You have no clue how to relate to the younger generation who now makes up your workforce. How we do what we do today is completely different from how we did what we did just last year, and he was sticking to his knowledge from 20 years ago.

He was very close-minded to any insights different from his own, and unless he catches a vision and the value of embracing change, he will continue to cycle downward in his profession. Change and the fear of change hits us in our personal lives, right, just as much as it does in our professional lives. I'm raising my sixth child, and guess what, it's completely different from my first, my second, my third, my fourth, and my fifth. You can never say as a parent there, done that, I got this. Rinse and repeat? There's no rinse and repeat with kids.

Each child is different. We must always be learning in our personal and our professional lives. Each work situation is different. Each leader we work with is different. Each coworker is different. We must become fearless and agile and open and willing to embrace the change that is all around us.

QUICK RECAP

Now, let's take a minute and review key messages we learned in this chapter. In this chapter, we learned why we tend to fear and avoid change, skills to help us identify where the fear is coming from so we can face it head on, and the value of accepting and embracing change.

Adapting and learning from change is key to staying relevant in our professions. Stay tuned as in my next chapter, I'll share teachings on how the best way to deal with unplanned change is by living daily with planned change. I know it sounds crazy, but hang out with me and you'll learn a bit more how this all looks.

PREPARE FOR UNEXPECTED CHANGE BY LIVING A LIFE OF PLANNED CHANGE

Welcome back. In this chapter, we will learn how to prepare for unexpected change by living daily with planned change. We will be learning the differences between planned and unplanned change, we'll review how living a life of planned change will keep us agile and flexible and more ready to accept unexpected change that comes our way. I'll touch on the power of having a growth mindset.

We will learn an acronym that helps us prioritise what areas of our lives we should focus on for planned change. Then, I'll wrap up this chapter with tactics that help us accomplish and follow through on the areas of planned change that we identify for ourselves.

Planned Change vs. Unplanned Change

So what is planned change versus unplanned change. Well planned change is what we do to ourselves. I know, crazy sauce. Planned change is living a life of constant goal setting to keep ourselves growing and learning. This is the part of living a life as an active adult learner we talked about in the previous chapter, on purpose work around developing new skills and character traits, always focus on improving our education and our professional skill sets.

Achieving goals gives us the personal confidence boost we need because confidence overpowers fears, right. Then we got this feeling, I can do anything is a stronger emotion than the fear that tells us to resist and avoid change.

POWER WORD: GROW

I've designed our next teachings regarding this topic of planned change around three power words, grow, prep, and push. I know it sounds a bit odd, but hang with me and it will all start to make sense. Our first power word grows reminds us to always look at change with a growth mindset. Let's take a few minutes and quickly review the characteristics of both a fixed and growth mindset to provide greater clarity.

A growth mindset believes intelligence and talents can be developed, seeks for and values feedback, embraces challenges, sees other's success as inspirational. A fixed mindset believes intelligence and talents are fixed, views feedback as criticism, avoids challenges, and feels threatened by others' success. Some of us might find ourselves somewhere in the middle and that's okay.

The purpose of understanding the difference between a growth and a fixed mindset in relation to planned change or goal setting is to recognize that for us to progress and move forward, we first have to have our heads in the right place. If you see yourself more towards a fixed mindset, it will be harder for you to open your mind to change.

POWER WORD: PREP

Now, let's move on to our second power word, prep. Now we may have an open mindset and be willing to change, but if our actions and behaviours don't change, nothing changes. I chose prep as my power word for two reasons. First, it reminds us that on-purpose plan setting is preparing us for change, and when it's used as an acronym, it helps to teach in which areas we should prioritise our planned goals for greatest positive impact. P, personal, our relationships. E, emotional intelligence. P, professional.

Now, let's go a bit deeper in each of these areas. Personal. Personal most often shows up in becoming physically stronger and more healthy. Our personal health must be first in our goal setting priorities. While goals in this personal category often show up with better eating habits and becoming stronger, it can also show up in goals that help us improve our coping skills that help with anxiety or depression or even strengthen spiritual connections. Relationship is next on the list. Nothing impacts us or throws us more off balance than when a relationship with one close to us is at odds. These challenges impact all areas of our lives.

Disruptions in personal relationships will show up in our work attitudes and behaviours. Planned change in this area might show up as spending more time with a significant other, parent, child or friend, providing service to one in need or even repairing a broken relationship. If a new social network is needed or desire for a change of friends, these too fall into this category. Now, the E in our acronym, emotional intelligence. Emotional intelligence is the capacity to be aware of, control, and express one's emotions and to handle interpersonal relationships judiciously and empathetically.

Emotional intelligence is a key ingredient to both personal and professional success. It guides our thinking and our behaviours. Skills in this area are what best help us manage and adjust our emotions to adapt to new and changing environments. Emotional intelligence certainly holds a place of relevance in our goal setting priorities. And the last in our list of goal setting priorities is professional.

Professional goals might show up as learning new skill sets to stay current in your industry, build out your client base by using new and different techniques not tried previously. Goal setting will show up unique for each of us based on our profession or the industries we work in.

POWER WORD: PUSH

Our next power word is PUSH. The word PUSH represents proven ways we can PUSH through to greater goal accomplishments. This word also breaks down as an acronym that teaches essential pieces of goal setting that most often get missed. And when they do get missed, we will typically fail at attaining the goal we set. These tactics are ones that I've identified both in my personal experience and through my years of leading and coaching others.

I coined them into an acronym for easy remembering. These tactics show to be the greatest help in accomplishing our goals. P reminds us to prioritise our focus. U, use what you've got. S, simplify the plan. And H, have fun. Now let's take each a bit deeper. P stands for prioritising our focus. The Pareto principle, or the 80/20 rule, teaches that most often we spend 80% of our time doing things that contribute only 20% towards our goals and only 20% of the time doing the vital stuff that contributes 80% of the results. We need to identify what helps the most towards accomplishing the goals and focus more of our time in this area. When we do this, we accomplish more in less time. I often find myself creating to-do lists and then more to-do lists to help me stay on track with the original to-do list I created. I know, I'm one of those.

It may sound like a sound practice, but because I spend so much time on my list, I often see myself pushing off the work that is more valuable and more impactful towards attaining my goal. So that might be an example of spending too much time in the 20% space instead of staying focused on the 80% priority, which is the actual work, the 80% area that truly creates change. Now, moving on, U for use what you've got reminds us to lean on our strengths and already established habits.

So an example of this might be if your goal is to learn a new language and if you are already in the habit of listening to talk radio or podcasts during your commute to work, just change it up and start listening to foreign language lessons instead. If you are social and outgoing and have a large network of friends, include a handful of them as accountability partners, people you can report your progress to and cheer you on in the work. Often, we try to push through hard goals all by ourselves and we miss the opportunity to have coaches and cheerleaders helping us along.

If your life is already embraced in technology, you enjoy having the latest and greatest tools and toys that technology provides, then find the right app, the tracker, the social network support group, or any other tech-enabled tool to help you in the work. Basically, use the skills you already have, as well as habits you've already established to help you on your journey of accomplishing your goals. Use what you've got. Moving on with our acronym, next is to simplify the plan, S. One way to keep it simple is to build out your plan around what has already been proven to work. Don't try to reinvent the wheel or over complicate your plan. If the goal is health-focused, find a plan that has been successful for others or recommended by your doctor.

Don't try and build your own diet plan. Stick to tested principles. If you are feeling overwhelmed, identify which part of the work is creating the stress, and then break it down and identify simple alternatives. Always remember don't push too hard or too fast. Break down large goals into small and simple steps. Then tackle those one at a time. When planning out your goal, think first about how much you can handle, then lowball it. Small and simple steps are the key to accomplishing the largest of goals. Okay, now to wrap up our acronym. He reminds us to have fun. What I mean by this is seek out what you enjoy and make that part of the plan.

For example, if you've never really been a gym junkie before, setting a goal to go to gym all of a sudden, not going to happen. This is where you need to seek out what is fun for you, what you enjoy doing, and incorporate the fun into the plan. I love to jump on the trampoline. I know, crazy. I put on my earphones, some Van Halen and Scorpions, and jump to my heart's intent. When it comes to physical exercise goals, there's so many fun ways to accomplish them, such as hiking in the mountains, walking with a group of friends, and competitive contests between friends. No matter how it shows up for you, make sure you're having fun in the process.

Now, if your goal is built around a work project, commit to the portions you enjoy and that you're good at. Delegate or sub out to others the work you don't enjoy. You will have a much better chance of success going this route. Remember, if you're having fun, enjoying what you're doing, then the odds of reaching your goals will be much higher.

QUICK RECAP

That wraps up our learnings around my power words of GROW, PREP, and PUSH. These tactics have been proven to help with greater goal accomplishments. To recap our learnings in this chapter, we learned that planned change or, in other words, ongoing personal goal setting is one of the best skills available to prepare us and ground us when unplanned change is thrown our way.

We learned the power words of GROW, PREP, and PUSH to remind us of the importance of having a growth mindset. PREP reminded us to prepare for change and to prioritise the areas we set our planned change goals in. And the tactics taught through our acronym of PUSH helps us push through our goals for greater accomplishment.

NAVIGATING THE CHALLENGES OF CHANGE IN YOUR WORK ENVIRONMENT

Changes in our work environments are among the top life stressors that we experience. Because of this, it's important that we have a clear lens on what type of changes to expect and that we have the skills necessary to help us navigate through and around these changes.

In this chapter, I'll review the top five most common changes in the workplace. We'll look at the difference in people's first instincts when they are first confronted with change, and we'll learn the three most important skills to help us navigate change in our work environments.

FAST PACES OF CHANGE

Expectations are increasing. New and creative ideas are always being implemented. The change of younger generations replacing older generations brings on its own packet of change as we previously mentioned. By the way, there's another great Amazon Book that compliments the teachings in this chapter. It helps us better understand the changing demographics, baby boomers, millennials, gen-Zs, gen-X that are coming in and out of the work environment.

You want to take some time to check it out, it'll be a great compliment to the learners in this chapter. But today, changes are happening at a pace never seen before. It comes at us with a faster and faster rate with the majority of it being tied to newer and advancing technologies. Planning and preparing for this change is what we've been learning in this Book. We need to stay fluid, agile. The more flexible and adaptable we are, the better chance we will have adapting to the change. Whenever I think of a person being agile or myself showing up that way, I picture this car lot dude, I'm sure he has a name.

Almost everyone has become acquainted with him as he waves to us boldly from most all car lots as we drive by. The change of the wind doesn't take him off Book. If we were to throw tennis balls at him, he would just bend, flex, float sideways for a bit, but he always comes back safely grounded. To me, our car lot dude is a great visualisation of being agile. He reminds us to flex and roll with the times of change.

TOP 5 CHANGES TO EXPECT IN THE WORKPLACE

Okay, back to the top workplace changes we can all expect. Studies show that the majority of us will experience these changes in our work environments and typically more than just once during our career spans. First on the list is leadership changes, most specifically who we directly report to. Then, team member changes, automation and machine learning, job responsibilities that are always changing the what and how we do what we do, culture improvements as executive leaders fight to offer the best environment for their employees, both to retain their current talent, but also to help attract new talent.

I'll now deep-dive into these five most common changes to provide better clarity. Leadership changes, who we directly report to, is the first on our list. When all is said and done, change that impacts who we directly report to can create the greatest pain point for us. We all know that relationships between leaders and employees take time. So when leadership change happens, it slows down the momentum of the team and adds stress and aches as a team works to relearn the expectations of their new leader. Leaders, especially newer-in-role leaders, are anxious to prove themselves early in the game. They have a tendency to jump into their new role and immediately start implementing change, some good, some not well thought through, and some just bad or off Book.

The intent of creating change with their new team typically is positive, but when this is introduced into the environment too soon, and what I mean by too soon is when change is made prior to making and finding time to connect with each employee, it brings too much stress and worry for the team. Next on our list of the most common changes is team member changes. Most organisations are experiencing a steady flow of employees in and out of our companies and in and out of our teams. The economy and the transition of younger generations into the workforce have the greatest impact on this. Data shows that Millennials and Gen Z age groupings are in and out of jobs and change careers many more times than any of the previous generations.

We do need to recognize that changes on our team can be good if the change helps to bring a diversity of race, gender, diversity of thought and of skill set. Diverse teams create a win-win for everyone. Next on our list of most common changes to expect in our places of work is the change that comes with automation and machine learning. Advancing technology brings with it not only new and upgraded hardware and software platforms, but opportunities to automate the work we do for higher production.

I think it's exciting to be living in the midst of all the fun technological advances taking place, but for others, it creates concern as automation has been gradually taking over jobs for decades. The introduction of machine learning has kicked the door wide open for explosive growth. Algorithms and tech products are so advanced, they can improve and code themselves. The jury is still out on how this will impact human jobs. But yes, there will be an impact of some sort. It may or may not show up in less opportunities for human skills, but it certainly supports my prior teaching of always living in a world of change.

We need to be active adult learners to keep up with advancing skills that will be required of us to support the changing technologies. I'm in a sidebar again as this is a great time to lift up Amazon's role IQ Assessments. Speaking of always ensuring we are on the cutting edge with our skill sets, Amazon's Role IQ assessments help to ensure our knowledge and skills are relevant to our roles by measuring our current proficiency. These tools offered by Amazon help you best identify a clear path for your career growth. And for leaders, it helps you quantify technology roles across your organisation to know whether you have the talent to meet your most critical objectives.

Next on our list of the most common workplace changes we can each expect is our job responsibilities, the how, what, and when of what we do in our jobs. Again, based on ever-evolving technology advancements, skill automation, and machine learning, our job responsibilities will continue to evolve and change based on how automation is showing up in our particular environments. Changing job responsibilities requires us to have growth mindsets to be fluid and agile employees. Just what we've been talking about, just a reminder that it is essential we learn to embrace change and embrace it sooner than later, right?

And the last of our top-five most common changes you will come across in your work environments are changes that impact your culture. We see high levels of attention across organisations, communities, even our social and political landscapes where planned culture change is taking place. It shows up in improved working conditions, improved and innovative benefits, and less rigidity around performance conversations.

As companies are realising that if we help our employees feel more comfortable and included at work, it's a win for everyone. So I just reviewed the five most common changes that we each can expect in our workplaces. But the one consistent thing about change is that change is always changing and reinventing itself into something new.

Curious vs. Judgmental Mindset

I'm now going to share the top three skills to help us best navigate these workplace changes. The first, and what I believe is the very most important, is living that life of planned change as we learned in chapter 3. The next skill best recognized to help us navigate workplace change shows up in our outlook. Now this skill complements my earlier teachings on having a growth mindset, but it goes a bit deeper when associated with change. We need to first identify how we ourselves react to change.

Is your first instinct to be curious or to be judgmental? Curious mindsets show up with a desire to listen to understand. They seek to find and comprehend the reasons behind the change. Curious minds ask questions rather than make assumptions. Curious mindsets show up more often as supporters of change. Those of us whose thoughts jump first to the judgmental side will immediately focus on the reasons why the change won't work. They immediately start poking holes in the plan. They fail to listen to the reason behind the change as they immediately start dissecting the plan to prove to others it won't work.

Here's another quick comparison to help you self-identify which direction you might typically lean towards. Curious minds are adept at exploring ideas around problems. When they come across obstacles in the work environments, they see them as opportunities to help find a solution for. Curious minds look for the positive and the benefits that change brings with it. People with judgmental mindsets focus first on the difficulties and problems at work.

They typically will withdraw or just shut down and pretend they are on board with all that's going on. But inside, they are really in a resistant frame of mind. Looking at change through the lens of curiosity is one of the major skill sets that helps us navigate change in our environments.

NAVIGATING CHANGE WITH YOUR HEAD, HEART, AND HANDS

Our next skillset after first living that life of planned change, then approaching change with a curious mindset comes with our head, heart, and hands approach. Let me walk through the meaning of this. First, the head. Head is the what of the change. What is to fully understand what the change consists of. What are the impacts on the company, on your teams, on yourself. You need to clearly understand what it entails, who it impacts, where and how the change is going to show up, and the impact it will make.

What also includes what were the problems or obstacles that this change was designed to circumvent. The key is to get all your questions answered around the what of the change. We need to fully understand this as it will help us better embrace the change. Next is the heart. The heart represents the motions of the change and is the why of the change. This is where you seek a deeper understanding as to why the change was made, why it was needed, why an organisation feels it's the right direction to take. Then the hands of change.

The hands represent action, reminding us to fully understand the how of the change. How does a company expect it to show up? How is it going to impact your current job responsibilities, and most importantly, how is it going to impact you? Again, keep asking questions. I have been teaching change management techniques for years and nothing shows it more impactful than aligning on the head, heart, and hands approach when dealing with change or when leading change. I want to take a minute to remind those who may be leaders of people.

If you are leading others through change, please remember how important it is for you, yourself, you must first grasp the head, heart, and hands of the change. If you, the leader, doesn't fully understand the why behind the change, if you don't agree or support the how of the change, you will create chaos amongst your teams. I worked with a team quite a few years back whose engagement survey showed a history of culture concerns within the department. After spending time with the team and the leaders of the team, I was able to identify the core cause that was creating such a break in their culture. It all boiled down to one leader who didn't believe in a past policy change that took place across the whole organisation.

He told a good story to those above him and to myself, but behind backs, he complained about the change. He never got on board. This negative influence festered amongst his direct reports and flowed down to each employee on the team. The entire department could not get past their frustrations with the policy change and it all flowed up to the leader having a fixed mindset and his refusal to listen to their reason behind the change.

It was a devastating experience to see an entire culture at risk all because the leader of their group wasn't able to flex and embrace change. So a reminder to people leaders, don't move forward initiating change until you yourself have your head, heart, and hands fully wrapped around the what, why, and how of the plan. It is essential for leading change.

QUICK RECAP

Time for a quick review of the key learnings in this chapter, navigating the challenges of change in your work environment. We learned about the five most common changes all will experience. We were reminded that the most important skill to prepare for change is by living a life of planned change. And then we learned the value of looking at change with curiosity and how to best navigate change in our work environments by using the head, heart, and hand approach.

If you work in an environment that isn't changing, but should to ensure they stay relevant and competitive within your industry, but the needed change isn't happening, then continue on with me to the next chapter as we will learn skills to help us become influencers of change.

BECOMING AN INFLUENCER FOR CHANGE

In this chapter, we are going to sidetrack a bit from our teachings around how best to embrace change and review how we can become change agents ourselves. There are times when we might work in an environment that is in need of change, but change isn't happening. This is when we, as an employee, need to step in to help lead the needed change by becoming a stronger influencer for positive change.

How cool would it be if we could just snap our fingers or call on some crazy cool superhero power that would cause all those around us to get on board to get it, to become willing partners and collaborators to help make needed change happen? But we all know influencing others towards change is a much mightier task than that.

In this chapter, we will be learning about what it takes to become a change agent, as well as a formula, to help us become that influencer for change. I know each of us would like this embedded within our own personal brands.

CHANGE AGENTS

First, let's touch on the definition of a change agent, another word for influencer of change. A change agent or agent of change is someone who promotes and enables change to happen within any group or organisation.

A successful change agent is a visionary who inspires others, creates enthusiasm, and either empowers their employees or, as an employee themselves, helps lead the charge for change with their peers.

BEHAVIOURS THAT INFLUENCE

Many have a desire to help lead change in our environments, but don't know where to begin. I came up with a formula a few years back when I was working with a frustrated leader. She truly wanted to make a difference for her and her team. But to accomplish what she wanted to do, she had to influence upwards, convince her direct supervisor and those above that the change was needed. As I coached her and worked with her through her situation a step at a time, this formula came to life in my head and quickly became a tool I reference often when coaching others in similar situations.

So our formula to become an influencer of change, B + C = A. I know. Simple, right? No, it's not just ABCs mixed around. I promise there is a method to this madness, starting with B. B represents behaviours. C speaks to consistency in those behaviours. And A stands for action, that after B and C are in place, then we have earned the right to act. So let's start with B. Our behaviours, how we are perceived. Do we have a positive brand? What do others see in us that would give them reason to follow us?

For those who want to dig a bit deeper into which workplace behaviours have the greatest impact for them professionally, I'll quickly go through a concept created quite some time ago by

Dennis Organ. He created a summary of workplace behaviours that show the strongest leaders of change. Organisational citizenship behaviours, commonly known as OCB. OCB is a person's voluntary commitment within an organisation or a company that is not part of his or her contractual task. OCBs contribute positively to overall organisational effectiveness. There are five behaviours that fall under the OCB definition. First is altruism.

What is this, you might ask? Well, this is a citizenship behaviour that shows when a person decides to help someone else without expecting anything in return or even any personal recognition for the work done. In a business setting, this would likely take the form of a worker choosing to help a coworker finish a project or a set of tasks, even though the work does not necessarily relate to what they need to get done in their own regular workday.

Next one is courtesy. It would be nice to think that most all humans exhibit common courtesy, but we all know the truth to that. It's basically being considerate and polite to those we work with. It can be as simple as watching our noise level if we are on the phone with a client so as not to disrupt others around us. The kindness of checking in on a coworker who is going through personal struggles. Very, very basic, but so often missed. The third one is sportsmanship. You might be thinking, say what? How does this show up at work? Well, this basic principle shows up when an employee decides to stay in good spirits, even when something does not go their way.

Refraining from complaining or gossiping also shows sportsmanship. Conscientiousness is best described in our work environments when employees go above and beyond. Coming into work early to finish a project, working to ensure team goals are exceeded for the quarter, developing a new way to approach a process or procedure, even when this duty is not outlined in their job description shows up as conscientiousness. Civic virtue is the last of the five behaviours most referenced as OCB. This is when we represent the company we are associated with in a positive light. This could occur within or outside of the business. It encourages a sense of community and strong interpersonal ties between coworkers.

This shows up when we speak favourably about the company we work for to those outside of it, participating in charity and community projects that company is involved in and even when we are engaged in planning or attending company-sanctioned social events. We just learned that the first part of our equation is built around having the right workplace behaviours, behaviours that lift your personal brand and help gain respect of all those you work for and with. The leader I mentioned earlier who I was working with when I coined this formula, believe it or not, she struggled in this area. She herself did not show up with the best of behaviours, which negatively impacted her personal brand and was seen as someone who made everything about herself.

Because of this, her journey to become an influencer of change was longer than most as she had to first focus on rebuilding and rebranding who she was and how she showed up. Having to go through a rebranding process can be done, but it is certainly a longer journey requiring personal change.

CONSISTENCY IN BEHAVIOURS

Okay, moving on. The next part of our formula is C. We need to add C to our B here. C shows up as consistency represents consistency in our personal values, work ethics, and behaviours. Showing up consistently in our work ethics and our behaviours shows that we are predictable and this then transitions into being seen as genuine and it shows to others we can be trusted. No matter what the situation, others want to know the one they trust is an influencer who is transparent and genuine in their interactions with others.

This is built through being consistent in how and what we do and say, and more specifically, in who we are. So back to our formula. We've now added C to our B, consistency to our behaviours, and this together gives us the right to act, and yes, A = action. With a positive personal brand and consistent and respective behaviours at work, we can now move forward working to implement change.

TAKING ACTION

As you move forward with action, to help implement needed change in your work environment, here are some key areas to focus on for greatest impact, introduce new perspectives for consideration, seek insights, gain supporting and opposing views from teammates, challenge the current state of the business by evaluating needs and helping to identify where change is needed.

Change agents help to harmonise and align leadership. They activate commitment and lead change within their peer group as they support the businesses' case for change. Now if you find yourself in an environment where change is needed, but nothing is being done about it, this is where you can and need to be the disruptor. A good disruptor, a disruptor for positive change. Let's review a few simple steps to initiate new change. First, identify the problem. Second, seek and listen to insights from others, or in other words, do research to find a solution by gathering diverse points of view and then combining with your own ideas, identify the solution. Third, present ideas for change and your recommended solutions through the right channels.

And last, but most importantly, if your ideas were turned down or not openly accepted, don't give up. Continue the drive for change. Circle back and rethink your solutions, finetune them and present again. Find stories to share of similar situations where similar solves made a difference. Bring others along with you to present your ideas to share their lens on the situation. The key is if the need is a must for your team or company to stay relevant in this crazy world of change, then don't give up.

Okay, now I know this concept is pretty basic and there may be some thoughts out there of well, no duh, but I want you to slow down and stop and think, which step is most often missed? The second one, right. When we desire to be an influencer for change, we present our solutions, our thoughts, we've got this right, we know the answers. Wrong. Often, we fail to slow down and gather insights from the entire team member getting diverse points of view, diverse thoughts, and bring those into the recommended solution. This is why most leaders fail to listen to our recommendations of solutions because a solution does not fit the entire team's needs.

QUICK RECAP

Let's do a short review of the learnings we discussed in this chapter. We reviewed how important it is for companies to be evolving and changing to ensure they stay relevant in the competitive landscapes, but the most important message from this chapter is if your company is not changing as it should, then employees can and should become influencers for change.

In this chapter, I reviewed a formula to follow to help you become that influencer. B + C = A, pretty basic. Consistency and positive behaviours gives each of us the right to take action to help influence our peer group and the leaders above us for positive change.

CONCLUSION

Always remember, knowledge breeds confidence, and confidence overcomes our fear of change. Let's take a couple minutes and recap what we've learned in this Book. We learned the value of embracing change. We learned to prepare for unexpected change by living with planned change. We learned about the most common workplace changes and skills to help navigate through those changes. We learned skills to help us become influencers for change. This brings us to the end of our Book.

Thank you for joining me on this journey. I hope you enjoyed it as much as I did creating it. Remember, always living a life as an active adult learner is a key to helping to stay relevant in our careers. Amazon has many great Books available to help each of us.

www.ingramcontent.com/pod-product-compliance
Lightning Source LLC
Chambersburg PA
CBHW071144220526
45467CB00015B/1892

* 9 7 9 8 3 9 1 0 4 8 6 7 1 *